Timing
The Market

**Debunking the Myth of
Time in the Market as
the Best Investment
Strategy**

Heather Cullen

DISCLAIMER

Dedication

To my wonderful children

Kim and Simon

Acknowledgements

I would like to thank Philip and Bob for their invaluable help in checking my backtesting.

Thank you!

**Markets are never wrong,
but opinions often are.**

Jesse Livermore

(The Original Wolf of Wall Street)

Contents

Introduction   1

Ch 1. You Heard It From The Herd   3

Ch 2. Missing The 10 Best Days   25

Ch 3. Can We Time the Market?   45

Ch 4. Market Timing: How Did It Go?   57

About the Author   65

Books by this Author   69

Contact the Author   71

HeatherCullen.com

Introduction

There is no shortage of advice from financial experts, yet the sad fact is that most of these experts have a dismal record and fail to beat the market. However, that doesn't stop them giving advice to others, and many people follow their recommendations to their detriment.

The most prevalent myth is that 'buy and hold' for the long term is the best, most profitable strategy. We are repeatedly warned that timing the market, getting out when it is going down and buying in again when it is going up, is impossible. We are told that timing the market is a failed strategy so we shouldn't do it, and instead stay fully invested, through good times and bad.

But here's the thing about that advice: It is wrong! Timing the market is not only possible, but gives much better results than riding out bear markets, as you will see in the results. Hard to believe? Yes, but after you have read this book, you will never follow such bad advice again. You will know a simple way to time your market exits and entries which will bring you better profits than staying in through the losses.

Ch 1. Heard From The Herd

'You can't time the market' say the experts, *'It's time IN the market that makes the money'*. You've probably heard it hundreds of times, in books, websites, news articles. But is it true?

Since the end of the bull market early in 2022, we have had hundreds of 'market experts' lined up to scare us into staying in the stock market and to not withdraw our money. The financial press has enthusiastically joined in, with pages full of 'wise' advice about the dire consequences of selling your investments when the market goes against you. You know the headlines:

Don't try to time the market – it doesn't work.

It's time in the market, not timing the market.

The best strategy is don't try to time the market.

Market timing fails as a money maker.

6 Reasons why market timing is for suckers.

Good investors stay in for the long term.

Buy and hold is the wisest thing to do.

Studies show that market timing doesn't work.

These are actual headlines, and they are all by respected commentators that millions of people follow like CNBC, Yahoo, Investopedia, Motley

Fool, Seeking Alpha, JP Morgan, several major banks, Forbes, and many others.

Financial advisers are all very keen for you to stay fully invested even when you are losing money. Why? Because they don't make any money when you are sitting on the sidelines with your capital in cash. There's no advantage to them in that. So, they come up with reasons you should ride out the storm. It's almost as though they were trying to frighten you into staying in the market.

Of course, everybody 'knows' that the 'experts' are right when they say, '***it's time in the market not timing the market'***. It is commonly accepted wisdom, and anyone who goes against the tide of popular opinion gets very little traction in the press or anywhere else. But here's the thing about that advice: ***it's all wrong***, as we'll see.

Staying in the market does NOT produce better results for the investor. It definitely produces better results for the market experts who handle your money and charge you for the privilege, but worse results for you as an investor.

The Echo Chamber

At this point you will probably have a healthy dose of skepticism about that claim. After all, if financial advisers, bank chairmen, the financial press, and investment gurus all tell you that that is right then surely it **must** be right, mustn't it? After all, they are the experts, and they all agree with each other. There's a consensus. Most investors trustingly believe them and hand their money over to these experts to look after, so surely, they can't be wrong.

Yet they **are** wrong. OK, some cynicism here is totally understandable. After all, who am I to challenge expert advice and recommendations? So about me. I am not a financial adviser, and I don't work for, and am not affiliated with, anyone except me. For the last 25 years I have been trading the stock market, and have written several books, but more of that later.

I am afraid that I'm a bit of a nerd and love debunking myths. I have a mathematical / statistical background and I was in IT for most of my working life until I stopped working for other people almost 20 years ago and started my own business.

One of the things both mathematical statistics and IT teach you to do is *look at what is actually there,* not what you think is there or what someone has told you is there or what *should* be there. In other words, if someone tells you that something is true, then before you act on it you need to check out the truth of the statement for yourself. So, I applied my skepticism to the stock market advice about market timing and went in search of the truth.

So, let's recap: this is the advice we've been given, and this is what we are going to do:

➢ **Buy and hold is the best strategy.** We look at the data to find out if it supports the theory and answers the question: Do investors who stay in the market through all events really do better than those who time their entries and exits?

➢ **Studies show market timing doesn't work.** Many studies are said to say this, but do they really? We'll look at those studies and see if they actually prove what they say they do.

Data and Replicability

One of the great things about researching the stock market is the amount of data that is publicly and easily available. You can go back 100 years in some cases, so there is no lack of data to analyze. It's the opposite, really.

The amount of data is enormous, and once you start going back decades the spreadsheets can get ridiculously huge and unwieldy. But that is just a minor issue. The main advantage is that:

The data availability means that any conclusions that I draw can be replicated by anyone willing to put in the time and effort, and the replicability of results is the basis of the scientific method.

This is a 'Short Read'

After writing four full-sized books, and having lots of questions and comments from readers, I realized that sometimes people just want to know about a single topic without having to wade through an entire book. Sometimes they just need a refresher on a specific subject but can't remember exactly where they read it. To address this need, I decided to write short books on individual topics in the stock market. I selected the topics based on what I got the most questions about.

This book is the first 'short read' to be published and is part of the One Hour Expert series. The information covered is too much for a simple report, but the scope is too limited for a full-sized book. It's more like a short story rather than a novel or a newspaper article. These books are designed to be read in an hour or so, although you may want to come back and reread particular parts of it.

Can We Time the Market?

Halfway through this book, after you have looked at the results you will probably throw your hands up in despair and decide never to believe a financial 'expert' ever again. You'll think*: If their advice doesn't work what am I expected to do?*

Fear not, I am not going to leave you with no hope and nowhere to go. I will show you a very, very simple way to time the market that beats all the experts, backtested for 30 years. It's really easy, takes hardly any time and it doesn't cost anything at all.

So, here's what we are going to do in this book. First, we will look at the most commonly cited piece of advice that says staying in the market through thick and thin is the best strategy.

I'll look at market data going back 30 years and show you how the studies have told a little bit of the truth but left out a lot of very important results which have a huge effect on your investment results. Then, we'll look at **if** and **how** we can time the market. The big question is*:*

Is there a way we can time the market safely and effectively?

The good news is, yes, absolutely, there is. There are several ways you can do this (and this is what my series In The Money is about) but I'll show you one very simple way that you can tell when to get out of the market and when to get back in, and which makes an enormous increase in your portfolio returns.

There are no "gotcha's" about any of this, it is an easy strategy you can easily do yourself using one of the many free charting tools available and you don't have to subscribe to anything to be able to implement it. My blog, **HeatherCullen.com/blog** is free and open to anyone, you don't even have to register unless you wish to be notified when there is an update.

So, let's start our investigation. Stock markets are not made up simply of stocks and companies, but of people who are deciding to buy and sell these stocks. Their decisions are what makes the market go up or down, and millions upon millions of these decisions are being made every day.

The Law of Large Numbers

Believe it or not there is a theorem called the **Law of Large Numbers**. The name amused me during my university studies as it seemed more suited to a Monty Python skit.

If you were a billion, did you have to behave better than a million? Did hundreds get away with more bad behavior than thousands? I mused on such matters through many a dreary lecture.

The Law of Large Numbers basically says that as a sample size grows, its mean (average) gets closer to the average of the whole population. For example, if you throw a die each of the 6 sides has an equal probability of landing on top so if we threw the die, say, a million time the average would be very close to 3.5.

However, if you threw the die three times then the average of the three values would likely not be exactly 3.5, but the more you throw the die (i.e., the bigger your sample size), the closer the average will get to 3.5. But what does that have to do with the stock market?

➢ We can't tell from individual stocks what the market is doing. It is not a random sample (traders have *chosen* the stock) and the sample size is smaller than the whole market.

➤ The S&P 500 index is between 70% and 80% of the total U.S. stock market capitalization, so it is a large sample that it is representative of the market as a whole and is commonly used as a benchmark for market performance.

The S&P 500 is an index (SPX) and can't be traded, but there is an ETF (Exchange Trade Fund) code SPY which mirrors SPX. It started in 1993, so we have 30 years of real data that we can analyze. We are going to use this as the basis of our first investigation.

So that's HOW we are going to do it, but it's people, not stocks, who make up the market. We'll start by looking at how people behave when making financial decisions.

Prospect Theory

Investing is all about profits and losses. Investors hope that their profits will be large and their losses small. But it is actions, not hope, that determine their results.

Investors can't blame everything on the experts. The experts don't have the last say, we - the individual investors - do. It is the investor who is making the decision to stay in the market, even while losses are mounting. No one is standing over us making us make the decisions. We're free agents.

So why do we make decisions that are clearly against sense and logic? Here we have to look at science to help us understand what is happening, and why people take actions that are often to their detriment.

There have been many studies about human behavior in decision-making, and **Prospect Theory** is the one that I think has the most relevance to investors. It is about how people assess their losses and gains.

While we love to think of humans, especially ourselves, as rational beings, this isn't actually the case: our behavior in making financial decisions is often quite the **opposite** of rational.

One of the reasons for irrational decisions is that people feel their losses much more than they feel a gain of the same size.

For example, the pain of making a loss of $10,000 might only be matched by the pleasure of making a profit of $20,000. Illogical, yes, but that's what many people feel.

Let's look at an actual example from one of the studies. Suppose you are presented with two scenarios about profits and losses, and you have to decide which choice you are going to make in each scenario:

> ➢ Scenario 1: You have a 100% chance to make a profit of $450 OR a 50% chance to make a profit of $1,000.

> ➢ Scenario 2: You have a 100% chance to make a loss of $500 OR a 50% chance to make a loss of $1,100.

What would be your decision? You might think that it depended on the person, and that some people are risk averse so they would choose the first option in both cases whereas people who have a higher tolerance for risk would go for the second option in each case. That seems logical. However, that's not what actually happened.

What did most people decide? In the first scenario, where they either made a certain profit of $450 or had a 50% chance of a profit of $1,000 they were *risk averse.* They chose a certain profit of $450 over the 50% chance of $1,000. But here is where it gets interesting.

In the second scenario, where they either made a certain loss of $500 or a 50% chance of a loss of

$1,100 then they became **risk-seeking** and chose the 50% chance of a loss of $1,100.

What would you have decided? I'm afraid that I went along with the herd, straight down the line, although I hesitated more about the second scenario than the first. In the first scenario I was risk averse in profits (*after all, who doesn't want a guaranteed $450?*), and then I was risk-seeking in losses (*after all, I might not make any loss at all, whereas if I choose the $500 loss then I'm locking in a definite loss.*)

Does this have an effect on how people trade?

Absolutely.

Investors will settle for less risky stocks with an expected smaller profit knowing that they are a 'sure thing', hence the emphasis on 'blue chip' or 'quality' or 'dividend' stocks.

They don't want to invest in little startups that, while they may have a chance of becoming the next Apple or Google and making an enormous profit, also have a significant chance of crashing and burning. However, when they come to selling their investments, it is a different story. When the market is going against them, and things are heading south there is a reluctance to sell and 'crystallize' their losses. As Alexander Pope said:

Hope springs eternal in the human breast.

Investors hope that the losses will only be temporary, that it is just a market aberration and that soon things will start heading north again and it may yet turn into a profitable trade. So, they hang on to their losing investments.

There's an oft quoted, and extremely irritating, market saying: *'You haven't lost until you've sold'*. In other words, if you want to, you can pretend to yourself that your holdings are worth more than the market is prepared to pay for them and that you haven't really made a loss. The correct term for this is self-delusion, and I'm always surprised when apparently rational people say it to me.

It's not clear whether the following quote comes from John Maynard Keynes or Gary Shilling (it's disputed) but no matter who said it, it is very relevant:

**The market can stay irrational
longer than you can stay solvent.**

You may think that your investments should be worth a lot more than the market is prepared to pay for them, and you may very well be right. But you don't have any idea if or when the market is going to agree with you.

The Sunk Cost Fallacy

The Oxford dictionary defines the sunk cost fallacy as:

The phenomenon whereby a person is reluctant to abandon a strategy or course of action because they have invested heavily in it, even when it is clear that abandonment would be more beneficial.

The sunk cost fallacy neatly dovetails with Prospect Theory. Once investors have selected a stock or an ETF, become personally attached to it, often becoming quite enamored with it.

They have invested part of themselves, as well as their money. Typically, they feel that they need to sell it for more than they paid because if they sell at a loss, it will mean that they were wrong, and people don't like to be wrong.

Consequently, if the price drops below their buying price they are reluctant to part with it. They 'know' that it is worth more. There's a mental block about selling it.

They hang onto their losing investment.

As investors sit on potential losses, just as Prospect Theory predicts, they become risk-seeking and grab at any possibility of avoiding the pain of a loss, even when it is clear that there is a risk of even greater losses. Like the people in the study, they are hoping that it might not happen.

This leads to the investor behavior of **buying the dip**, where an investor keeps on buying as the stock goes down, because *'it becomes more and more of a bargain'*.

This is called 'doubling down' and the expectation is that when the stock recovers, they will recover their losses more quickly.

This is the essence of a strategy called 'dollar cost averaging' where you buy at regular intervals to spread out your purchases. Proponents of this approach point out that you would have bought most of your stock at the lower prices.

Very true – but they could keep getting lower and lower. What if the stock never recovers? It happens.

Many stocks which have cratered, here are a couple of stocks that were once the bluest of 'blue chip' or 'quality' stocks.

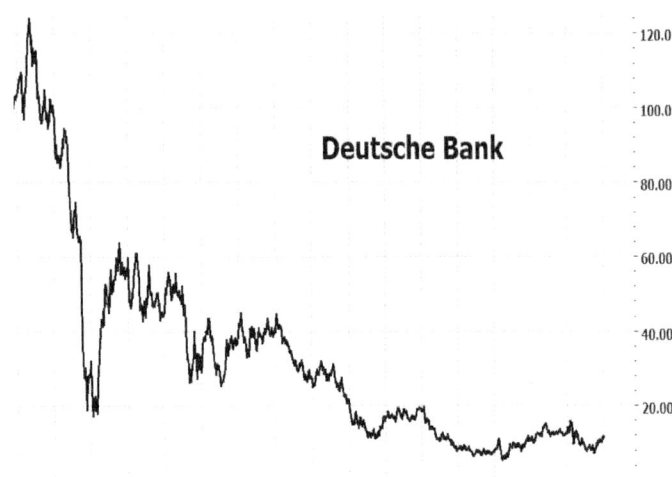

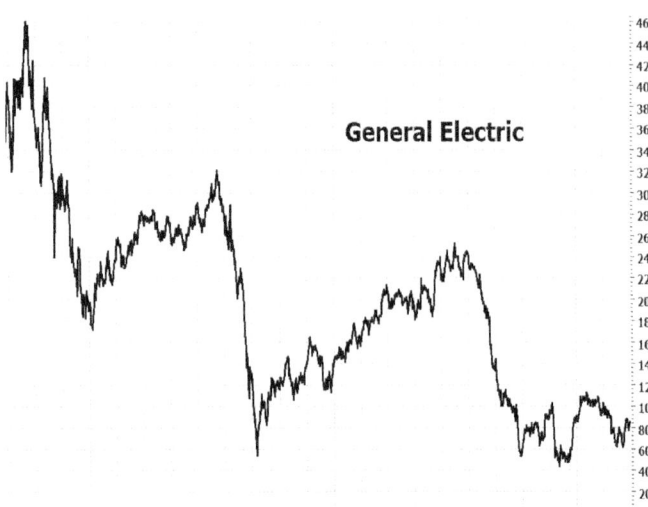

18

And of course, currently we have watched the rise and fall of bitcoin. Here's the chart for the last year:

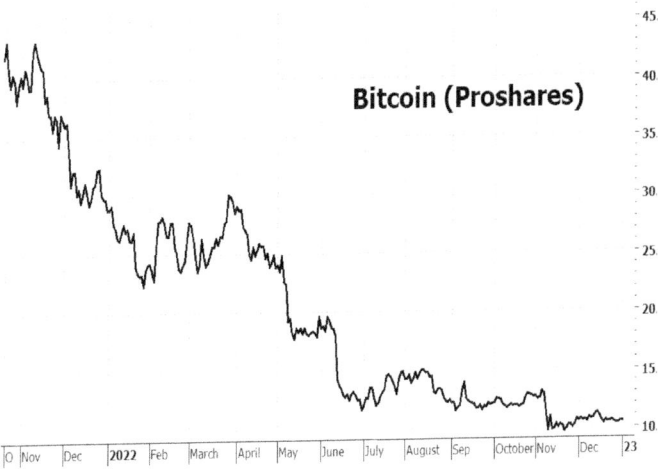

Buying the Dip

Buying the dip is often recommended because shares are 'cheap' and a 'bargain'. However, it is a strategy fraught with danger, often described as trying to 'catch a falling knife', which is not something anyone wants to do either in real life or in the stock market.

Imagine trying to catch the bottom of the market during the GFC (Great Financial Crisis), when stocks were getting cheaper and cheaper and at 'bargain prices':

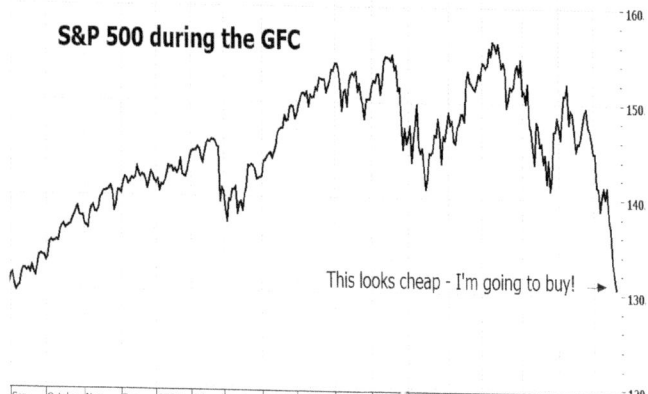

Let's say that we buy in January at $130. Should we be happy with our 'bargain' buy? Let's take a look six months later:

Now we can buy it for $120! That's got to be a bargain! Let's fast forward another three months:

It's so cheap! Only $90! It can't get any cheaper surely. I've got to buy some more! A few months later:

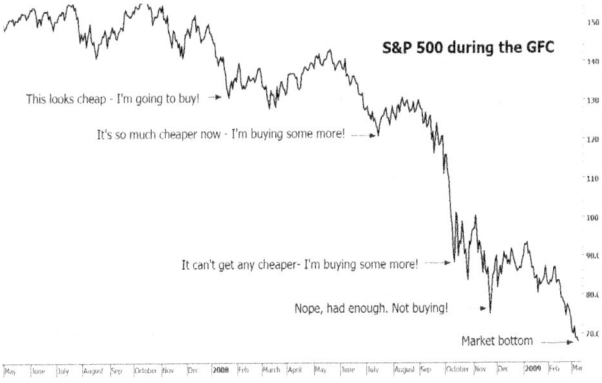

About this time, having watched the share price drop to $68 and their capital disappear before their eyes, disillusionment sets in. They don't like this game, and they are not playing any more. They capitulate. They sell at the bottom of the market.

Investor Psychology

Psychology is at play here too. The more an investor doubles down and invests more money, the more risk-seeking their behavior becomes, and the higher their losses can be.

Unfortunately, the decision to buy and hold has a bit of a cult-like status, both in traditional investing circles and more recently, with younger investors who started trading during the Covid lockdowns.

Financial firms call investors who follow this approach 'long term' or 'buy and hold' investors and the implication is that they are wiser investors than people who get in and out of the market.

In the trendier trading circles, like the Robinhood Markets, they are, admiringly, called 'diamond-hands'. The term signifies someone who can take the pressure, just as diamonds need high temperatures and pressure to form.

They are investors who can 'take the heat'. They are tough. They don't sell if their investment falls in value but hang on waiting for it to recover. Unfortunately, many 'diamond hands' were severely burned by the GameStop fiasco. As we saw previously, just because a stock has dropped significantly there is no guarantee that it is ever going to recover.

Conversely, there are 'Paper Hands', investors who are afraid of losses and sell as soon as there is even a slight price decrease. You may have heard of a trailing stop where you automatically get out of a trade when it goes against you.

For example, if you bought a stock at $100 you might place a stop loss at $98, congratulating yourself on not being able to lose more than 2% on the trade. If the stock drops to that level, it automatically gets sold.

A trailing stop means that your stop loss can move up if the stock price increases to always be $2 below the current price. If the stock increased to $104 your stop loss would then be set at $102.

The Problem with Trailing Stops

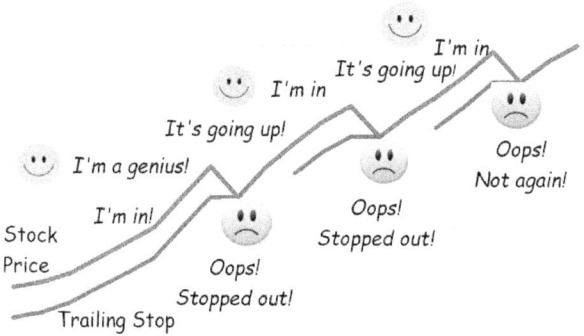

While this is often touted as a safe way to trade, if you don't set your stop to allow for normal price variations then it pretty well guarantees that you will sell your stock at the worst time just to watch it recover. The low-risk tolerance of 'paper hands' can deplete portfolios bit by bit.

Don't Be Part Of The Herd

There are a lot of myths and misconceptions in the market, with lots of people agreeing with each other in a stock market echo chamber. However, the stock market doesn't care about anyone's hypothesis or opinion and will do whatever it wants to do no matter what you think it *should* do.

The stock market will roll right over you no matter how many people agree with you.

Belonging to a herd is comfortable; as humans, we feel safe to have a lot of people agreeing with you. But, as we'll see, belonging to a herd that 'believes' in a market hypothesis without checking the actual figures guarantees that you won't perform as well as someone who looks for hard evidence and invests accordingly.

Ch 2. Missing the 10 Best Days

We're used to hearing variations on this warning from any number of financial advisers, banks, and investment houses:

Your portfolio can suffer heavily if you miss even a few of the best days in the market, and you never know when they're coming.
Best to stay fully invested at all times.

It sounds reasonable and most people believe it, but is it reasonable, and should they believe it?

Let's look at the motivation of the people giving this advice. Is there any reason why banks and money managers would have you believe that you should stay fully invested at all times? Why indeed?

Because it is in their interests.

You give them your money to invest, and they don't want to give it back anytime soon. They want as many 'funds under management' as they can get.

So, to make sure you leave it with them they frighten you with warnings like *'if you miss the 10 best days your profits will be halved or worse.'*

The **10 Best Days** is the myth most often cited by people urging you not to get out of the market when it is going against you. The theory is that if you miss the 10 best days of a year or a decade or any other time period then your profits will plummet.

The corollary that is drawn from this is that in order to win in the market an investor must stay fully invested at all times.

Before we get to the actual figures and debunk this myth, it is interesting to see the logical error in it. It is an excellent example of a **'non sequitur'**. This is a Latin expression meaning **'it does not follow'**. According to the Oxford dictionary, a non sequitur is:

A conclusion or statement that does not logically follow from the previous argument or statement.

There are different types of non sequiturs. There is a type called the 'fallacy of the undistributed middle' and the '10 Best Days' myth is an excellent example of this. It fails to follow logic and leads to an unfounded conclusion. For example, here are some non-sequiturs:

1. If someone owns a yacht, they are rich.
2. Elon Musk is rich.
3. Therefore, Elon Musk owns a yacht.

Now, I have absolutely no idea whether or not Elon Musk **does** own a yacht, but you can see the obvious fallacy in the argument. *It does not follow.* Another example is:

1. Pierre is very talented.
2. All musicians are talented.
3. Therefore, Pierre is a musician.

And even more absurdly:

1. Cats have 4 legs.
2. My dog has 4 legs.
3. Therefore, my dog must be a cat.

You can see that the first two statements are facts, but the last is a conclusion and in the case of this type of non sequitur it is an incorrect conclusion. It may sound logical, but by looking at some examples you can quickly see the absurdity. Let's look at the *time in the market* non sequitur.

The first two statements in this case are:

1. There are 10 days where the market goes up the most and makes the most profit.

2. If I miss those 10 days, then I will miss out on the best profits.

Both of these statements are correct: if you miss the days that the market goes up most you won't have increases that go with these up days. But the conclusion clearly doesn't follow logic:

3.   Therefore, I must stay fully invested.

Absurd, isn't it? Yet this is what these papers – and all the financial advice – are predicated on. It is a fallacious conclusion, but it is surprising how many people who should know better fall for it.

Even more absurd is the idea that somehow, we would know in advance that the market was going to have one of its 10 top days and get out the day before at close, wait out during the next day, then get in exactly on the close.

No one can predict when the market is going to have one of its 10 best days, so you will never know when to get out, but it does not follow that you had better stay invested just in case.

It is a completely ridiculous experimental design, yet it repeatedly gets trotted out as 'proof' that staying in the market whatever the market is doing is the right thing to do.

The 10 Best Days Studies

Financial advisers and other experts who give you this advice will cite studies that they say show that over the long term investors make money from staying in the market to avoid missing a handful of big one-day gains. There are quite a few studies that you can google:

- ➤ Putnam
- ➤ Bank of America
- ➤ Motley Fool
- ➤ JPMorgan
- ➤ Forbes
- ➤ NE Investments
- ➤ Javier Estrada

Some of these are big names, so you can see why they are not challenged, and why people take everything they say on face value. But let's actually **look** at the studies.

Most take different time periods, and most don't actually show their calculations or the source of their data, so you have to take their results on faith, and funnily enough, sometimes the same studies have different results depending on where you read them. But first, about how I checked their results.

I reviewed the studies to find out if there was enough information to enable me to check the dates and the source of the data (see heathercullen.com if you want a link). I then checked the results of those studies to make sure that their figures were correct, and whether they were using adjusted close figures which incorporate the dividends that had been paid during the period of the study.

Using data from various sources, and many spreadsheets, I concluded that in the main their figures were accurate. No surprises there, I didn't really expect them to be wrong.

The surprise was what they <u>didn't</u> mention!

The Putnam Study

One of the most widely quoted and referenced studies, and one of the most recently updated, is the Putnam study, which was updated in February 2022. It has been referenced in hundreds of articles on many different websites and in many articles and publications.

It is a very short paper, only 2 pages with very little information as most of the two pages are graphs. I don't have permission to reproduce it here, but you can easily see the original by googling: 'Putnam 10 best days 2022'. It is headed:

Time, not timing, is the best way to capitalize on stock market gains.

The subtitle goes on to explain:

By trying to predict the best time to buy and sell, you may miss the market's biggest gains.

The study looks at the S&P 500 index over the period 2007 – 2021, and the next heading concludes that you must:

Stay invested so you don't miss the market's best days.

The study starts with $10,000 invested in the S&P 500 at the start of 2007 and graphs what would happen to your account value if you missed the 10/20/30/40 best days. They conclude with the dire warning:

By staying fully invested over the past 15 years, you would have earned $24,753 more than someone who missed the market's 10 best days.

And they are absolutely right. Their figures are correct, other than a small anomaly about their claimed start date of 31st December 2006 (the market was not actually open on that day; it closed on the 29th of December and did not open again until January) but this caused only a minor difference.

So, let's look at **what** they are saying: if you somehow had the prescience to know that one of the 10 best days of the fifteen years was coming up (and this is before the fifteen year period has ended!) and got out for that one day and that one day only then you would have cut your profits by more than 50%. And they are right.

But with such a ridiculous premise, how can anyone take this study seriously? However, leaving that aside, even more interesting is what they leave out.

What They DON'T Say

The Putnam study starts with $10,000 invested on 31st Dec 2006. And then for the next 15 years they compare staying in the market at all times or missing the 10 best days. The results are:

- ➤ Stay fully invested: $45,235.
    - ○ (10.59% ROI annualized)
- ➤ Miss 10 best days: $20,466
    - ○ (4.89% ROI annualized)

The results look convincing, don't they? Who would want their ROI to be 4.89% when it could be 10.59%? It sounds like game, set and match for the financial advisers, doesn't it?

Enough evidence to take their advice and stay in the market through thick and thin? That's what most people think. But:

The BIG Question (that never gets asked)

The financial advisers and press assiduously avoid asking:

What would happen if we missed the 10 worst days?

Assuming that you had this marvelous foresight that could tell you what was going to happen the next day, wouldn't it be better used to get OUT of the market when one of the 10 worst days were coming up? How would that work?

Obviously, it is just as impossible to avoid the 10 worst days as it is to make sure you don't miss the 10 best days, so we are still looking at an absurd situation. But that's what everyone is quoting, so let's follow their rules and look at the results even though we know the basis of the paper is ludicrous.

We start with $10,000 on 31 Dec 2006 and for 15 years we:

> ➢ Stay fully invested: $45,235.
>> o (10.6% ROI annualized)
>
> ➢ Miss 10 best days: $20,466
>> o (4.9% ROI annualized)
>
> ➢ Miss 10 worst days: $106,775
>> o (17.1% ROI annualized)

Interesting, isn't it?

You always hear about missing the 10 best days, but you never hear about missing the 10 worst days, and they make much more of a difference.

You have to wonder – why do most financial advisers and the financial press not ask that question? Isn't it equally important?

As you can see above, if you can avoid the 10 worst days then you more than double your return. This is because losses ('drawdowns') on your account have quite a devastating effect. Recovering from losses is neither quick nor easy.

Most people think '*well, I've dropped 30% but no problem, the market will probably go back up 30% and I'll get it all back'.*

Nice idea – but unfortunately it is incorrect. If you lose 30% then the market needs to increase by 43% before you are back at breakeven. If you lose 50% of your account value, then the market has to double before you are at breakeven. Take a look at the table on the next page.

To many people these figures are a bit of a shock, but they emphasize the importance of avoiding losses as much as possible. If you avoid major losses (drawdowns) on your account, you don't have to spend time making up the losses and you are free to take advantage of the upside. Yet most financial advice is about missing out on the up days not the down days, which clearly have a MUCH bigger effect on your account balance.

Starting value	% Loss	$ Loss	Account Value	% to Breakeven
$10,000	10%	$1,000	$9,000	11%
$10,000	20%	$2,000	$8,000	25%
$10,000	30%	$3,000	$7,000	43%
$10,000	40%	$4,000	$6,000	67%
$10,000	50%	$5,000	$5,000	100%
$10,000	60%	$6,000	$4,000	150%
$10,000	70%	$7,000	$3,000	233%
$10,000	80%	$8,000	$2,000	400%
$10,000	90%	$9,000	$1,000	900%
$10,000	100%	$10,000	$0	

The Bank of America Study

Other studies showed similar dire effects on your account if you missed the best days. One frequently cited study is the 100-year Bank of America study:

Wednesday Mar 24, 2021

Looking at data going back to 1930, Bank of America found that if an investor missed the S&P 500's 10 best days each decade, the total return would stand at 28%. If, on the other hand, the investor held steady through the ups and downs, the return would have been 17,715%.

That sounds very impressive, doesn't it? Here's how the study was reported. The headline on CNBC said:

This chart shows why investors should never try to time the stock market.

The chart is not actually a chart (OK, being pedantic), but a table headed '**The difficulties of trying to time the market**' with the results in very small print. It is printed below.

(It is a bit hard to read but I wanted to use the actual table. You can google it to see it closer)

The difficulties of trying to time the market
Bank of America looked at the impact of missing the market's best and worst days each decade

Decade	Price return	Excluding worst 10 days per decade	Excluding best 10 days per decade	Excluding best/worst 10 days per decade
1930	-42%	39%	-79%	-50%
1940	35%	136%	-14%	51%
1950	257%	425%	167%	293%
1960	54%	107%	14%	54%
1970	17%	59%	-20%	8%
1980	227%	572%	108%	328%
1990	316%	526%	186%	330%
2000	-24%	57%	-62%	-21%
2010	190%	351%	95%	203%
2020	18%	125%	-33%	27%
Since 1930	17,715%	3,793,787%	28%	27,213%

Source: Bank of America, S&P 500 returns

CNBC

The article was headed with 3 Key Points, which are often the only bits that people read. What is selected as the key points determines what most readers are going to read, remember, and take away from the article.

Key Points

> - *Investors should avoid the impulse to time the market, new data from Bank of America shows.*

> - *Looking at data going back to 1930, the firm found that if an investor sat out the S&P 500's 10 best days per decade, total returns would be significantly lower than for investors who waited it out.*

> - *The market's best days typically follow the largest drops, meaning panic selling can lead to missed opportunities on the upside.*

Clearly, they are recommending staying in the market whatever is happening, and until you actually look at the data this seems reasonable When you look at the data in the table *in the report* you see quite a different story:

> - Staying invested for 100 years: **17,715%.**

> - Excluding best 10 days: **28%**

> - Excluding worst 10 days: **3,793,787%**

> - Excluding best 10 & worst 10: **27,213%**

Note that this data is taken directly from the table of results. The figures show that by sitting out the worst days you would have an increase of almost **4 million percent!** Not a result to be overlooked, one would have thought. You would not be aware of that from the headlines or the key points, as they totally ignore this incredible result. Graphically you can see the scale:

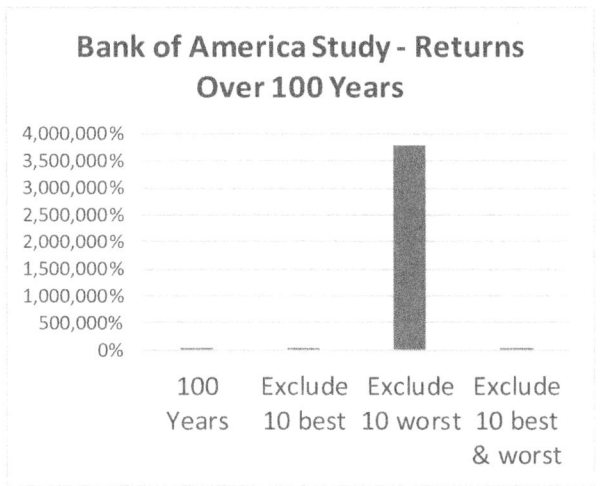

According to the Bank of America's own figures, excluding the 10 worst days gives you an enormous percentage return of 3.8 million%

That's right, an increase of 3,793,787%. Your original $10,000 would now be worth close to half a BILLION dollars, but they barely mention that and conclude:

Given the difficulty of precisely calling the peaks and troughs, the better bet is to simply stay in (sic) invested.

It is hard to understand why the headline and the key points miss such an important piece of information, but they do. It is harder to understand why they should make such an illogical conclusion as 'you have to remain invested'. One has to wonder why? Why hasn't this been challenged?

Ignore The Bad Advice

As we've noted it is impossible to predict the best 10 and worst 10 days, as we only know in hindsight after the end of the decade or the fifteen year time period. But what can we learn from this?

Definitely, ignore the advice about staying invested so that you don't miss the 10 best days. It is an absurd scenario. If we could predict the 10 best days, we could also predict the 10 worst days, and then look what our returns would be! We'd all have a private island with a chateau and a helicopter! (Pause for daydream – OK, back to reality).

It does, however, give us a clue about what to look for in our research. Here's a table that uses the Bank of America figures from the study and translates them into the effect on the account year by year.

Decade	Price Return	Excluding 10 best	Excluding 10 worst	Excluding 10 worst & 10 best
1930	-42%	39%	-79%	-50%
1940	35%	136%	-14%	51%
1950	257%	425%	167%	293%
1960	54%	107%	14%	54%
1970	17%	59%	-20%	8%
1980	227%	572%	108%	328%
1990	316%	526%	186%	330%
2000	-24%	57%	-62%	-21%
2010	190%	351%	95%	203%
2020	18%	125%	-33%	27%

We can notice something interesting:

The result from excluding the 10 best AND the 10 worst seem to be correlated with the market price return for that year.

The correlation is not perfect, but it is noticeable enough to be worth investigating. What could explain that? Is it that bear markets have a disproportionate effect on the results?

If we could avoid bear markets what would be the return on investment?

Unfortunately, I can't get the daily data that Bank of America used so I cannot analyze it.

I can, however, revisit the Putnam study where there is daily data and see if there was a similar effect.

Bears & the Putnam Study

Let's review the Putnam results before we delve deeper. The returns and annualized ROI were:

- ➢ Stay fully invested: **$45,235**
    - ▪ (10.66% ROI)
- ➢ Miss 10 best days: **$20,466**
    - ▪ (4.89% ROI)
- ➢ Miss 10 worst days: **$106,775**
    - ▪ (17.10% ROI)

And the dates of the study were 31st December 2006 to 31st December 2021. The first thing you notice about the dates are:

- ➢ It starts just before the GFC Bear Market
- ➢ It incorporates the Covid bear.
- ➢ It stops at the bull market top (Dec 2021)

Let's be kind and assume that these dates are just coincidences and not chosen, but what effect does it have on the results?

If we look at a chart of the time period, we note something interesting: 19 out of the 20 best / worst days occurred in a bear market.

On the next page is a graph with the 10 best days (above the X axis) and the 10 worst (below the X axis), with the bear markets marked with shaded boxes.

With the exception of one down day in August 2011 (and only the ninth worst day, not one of the big ones), all the big days occurred in a bear market.

What a coincidence! So, if we had avoided the big up days, we would probably have avoided the big down days as well. If we had avoided the bear markets, we'd be way in front!

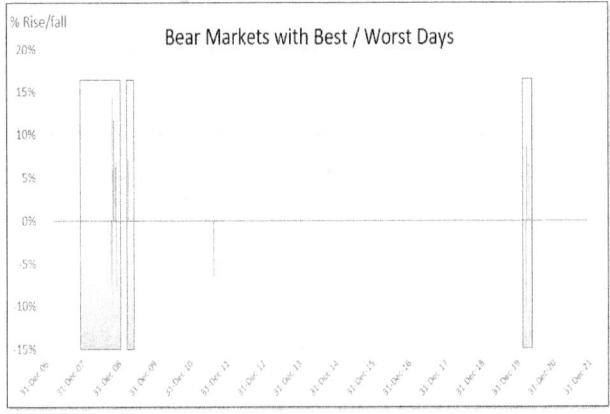

You see, the good and bad days tend to occur around the same time, as anyone with a nodding acquaintance with the stock market could tell you.

Here's the list of the best and worst days during the period of the study:

Order (big > small)	Date	Adjusted Close	% Rise	Date	Adjusted Close	% Fall
1	13-Oct-08	$101.35	14.5%	16-Mar-20	$239.85	-10.9%
2	28-Oct-08	$93.76	11.7%	15-Oct-08	$90.02	-9.8%
3	24-Mar-20	$243.15	9.1%	12-Mar-20	$248.11	-9.6%
4	13-Mar-20	$269.32	8.5%	01-Dec-08	$82.11	-8.9%
5	23-Mar-09	$82.22	7.2%	29-Sep-08	$111.38	-7.8%
6	24-Nov-08	$85.03	6.9%	09-Mar-20	$274.23	-7.8%
7	06-Apr-20	$264.86	6.7%	20-Nov-08	$75.45	-7.4%
8	13-Nov-08	$91.17	6.2%	09-Oct-08	$90.70	-7.0%
9	20-Oct-08	$98.81	6.0%	08-Aug-11	$112.26	-6.5%
10	10-Mar-09	$72.17	6.0%	19-Nov-08	$81.50	-6.4%

Big movements in one direction tend to occur close to big movements in the other direction, and the most volatile times are during bear markets. Yet, no one mentions that in the study or looks at the effects of holding through a bear market. You can see how close to each other they are. So, the logical next question is:

Is there a way we can avoid bear markets?

And if the answer is yes, then the next question will be:

What would our results be if we avoided bear markets?

This is what the rest of the book covers. In Ch. 3 Timing the Market, you will see how to avoid bear markets, and in Ch. 4 you will see what your results would have been if you had avoided the bear markets.

Ch 3. Can We Time the Market?

Bear markets start when the market drops 20% from its high and end when it rises 20% from its low. Obviously, we don't know the high or the low until afterwards, but the 20% buffer gives us enough space to work it out. The method I am going to show you here does not rely on hindsight but on simple observation.

Market Indexes

You will have heard of some market indexes like the Dow Jones Industrial Average, the S&P 500, and the Nasdaq. We are going to use the index that is generally considered to be the most representative of the U.S. stock market which is the S&P 500.

The index (code: SPX) is calculated using a weighted average of the stock prices of the companies included in the index, with each company's weight determined by its market capitalization.

Indexes can't be traded, but we can trade an ETF (Exchange Traded Fund) that tracks the performance of an index. SPY mirrors the S&P

500, and it is the largest and oldest ETF in the world, with assets under management of $300 billion. SPY is used as a proxy for the stock market.

Stock Charts

You are probably familiar with candlestick stock charts, but just in case you're not let's do a quick overview.

Charts show the price of the stock over time and are usually line graphs or candlestick graphs. Candlesticks are commonly used as they give the best illustration of what is actually happening with the stock price.

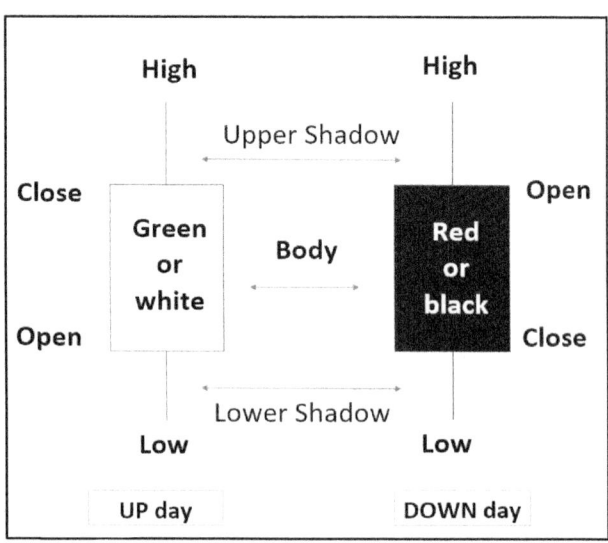

Each candlestick is based on the price action of stock or ETF during a time period, which could be a month, a week, a day, an hour or a minute, or any other time period you choose.

We are going to use charts with a daily candlestick. Candlesticks consists of a body and two shadows and shows the open / high / low / close price during the trading day and is green (or white) on an up day and red (or black) on a down day.

Stock charts are provided by most online broking platforms, but if they don't then you can use one of the many free ones that are available.

Some of these are excellent and if you do not already have access to charts then I suggest that you use Yahoo! finance charts. To find them just google 'yahoo finance spy chart'.

The SPY Daily Chart

Stock charts are very useful enabling you to see the price action over time for a stock or an ETF.

Although not strictly necessary for following this method of timing the market, it's way more fun if you can see what is going on so I encourage you to look at the charts and become familiar with them.

Below is the daily SPY chart for this year (2022) with the 10-day and 200-day simple moving averages (SMAs) on it.

Moving averages smooth out the 'noise' (the short term fluctuations) and make it easier for you to see the longer term trend.

Moving averages are calculated by taking the average of a specified number of days and moving with time.

For example, the value of the 20 day moving average is always the average of the previous 20 days. A simple moving average (SMA) gives equal weight to every day, whereas an exponential moving average (EMA) gives greater weight to the more recent dates. You don't have to worry about calculating a moving average, that is always done by your charting package based on the parameters that you choose.

Looking at the above chart we can see the 200 day SMA (the thick line) and the 10 day SMA (the thin line). The 200 day is smoother and less volatile than the 10-day SMA, which closely follows the price action.

The SMAs crossed over in February and again in late March / early April, and since that time the 10-day SMA has been underneath the 200-day SMA.

This is what happens in a market trending downwards. Short term moving averages are below the longer term ones.

Golden and Death Crosses

Although they are not necessary for this strategy it's good to know about some basic charting indicators and patterns.

Golden and Death crosses are when the shorter-term SMA (in this case the 10-day SMA) crosses over the longer-term SMA (the 200-day SMA).

> ➢ When the 10-day SMA crosses over the 200-day SMA to the upside this is called a golden cross, and it is a bullish signal.

➢ When the 10-day SMA crosses over the 200-day SMA to the downside this is called a death cross, and it is a bearish signal.

Here is a chart of SPY during the 2020 Covid bear market, with the death cross (bearish signal) and the golden cross (bullish signal).

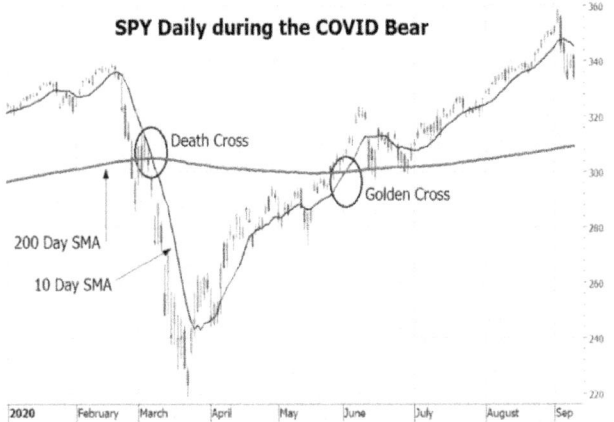

You can see that the Death cross came shortly after the market started going south (bearish) and the golden cross when it was going north again (bullish).

The Covid bear was the shortest and sharpest bear market on record, dropping 34% in 3 weeks. It was swift and deep, and if you were in the market, it would have been terrifying watching your account balance go down and down, not knowing when it was going to reach the bottom.

Because it was the shortest bear market ever, followed by a very sharp bull market, people who decided to sit tight regained their money within 6 months. This was unusual, as bear markets tend not to recover quickly.

In fact, Bank of America's figures show that it takes and average of 1,100 days to recover losses from a bear market. That's more than three years! But it can be much worse than that.

If you got into the market in 2000, you had to wait almost 13 years to get back to where you bought in. If you got into the market in 1996, then in 2009 the market was at the same level, and you hadn't made any money in fifteen years.

You can see the buy-and-hold strategy generally recommended by market gurus can be painful for a very long time, longer than most of our trading horizons. This is not what we want.

That's why we are looking at getting out at the start of a bear market and then getting back in again when it is over. Yes, the experts say it can't be done.

The experts are wrong. Look at this very simple strategy.

IN and OUT Signals

What we are going to do is very simple:

> ➢ When we enter a bear market we sell
>
> ➢ When we exit a bear market we buy back in

Simple, isn't it? Seems so obvious. How come no one has ever thought that before? *(I am joking, of course, many people have thought about it!)*

But how do we actually do this? And what exactly is a bear market anyway?

> **A bear market starts when the market drops 20% from its most recent high and ends when it rises 20% from its low.**

To be able to see this, you will need access to a chart or, at the very least, to daily SPY data. As discussed, your broker may provide charts, or you can access excellent free charts and data from Yahoo Finance.com

Start and End of a Bear Market

As we've noted, officially a bear market starts when the market is down 20% from its most recent high. If we look at the last 30 years, there have been 5 bear markets.

The first bear market was after 8 years, in 2001. I have chosen this as it shows a recovery that almost made it out of a bear market, only to drop further, reentering another bear market. Bear markets can be very difficult to predict.

The market high was on the first of September 2000, when SPY was trading at $152.50 (see first circle on the chart). The market started dropping, only stopping for a couple of bull traps in November 2000 and January 2001.

The bear threshold was $122 (How? $152.50 * 0.8) and SPY entered a bear market in March 2001 (second circle).

The market dropped to $110.39 then started climbing, but it did not climb out of bear territory.

The low of $110.39 was at the start of April, so the end of the bear market was when it traded over $132.47 (How? The low $110.39 * 1.2).

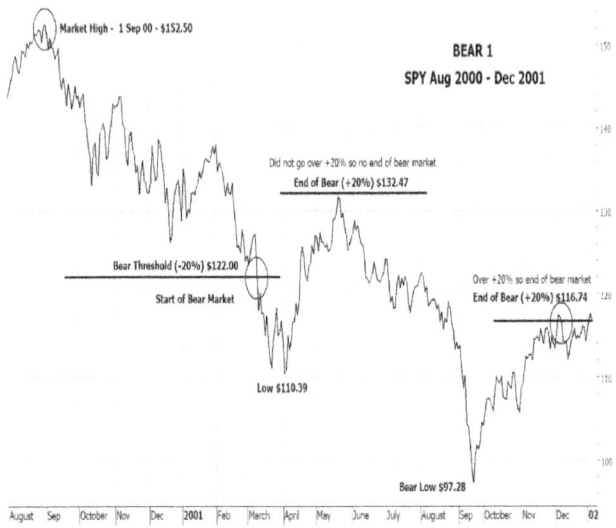

Market High - 1 Sep 00 - $152.50

BEAR 1

SPY Aug 2000 - Dec 2001

Did not go over +20% so no end of bear market
End of Bear (+20%) $132.47

Bear Threshold (-20%) $122.00

Start of Bear Market

Over +20% so end of bear market
End of Bear (+20%) $116.74

Low $110.39

Bear Low $97.28

August Sep October Nov Dec 2001 Feb March April May June July August Sep October Nov Dec 02

In late May it almost reached this level, didn't quite make it, then started to drop again. This time it went even lower, reaching $97.28 in September.

To end the bear market, SPY would have to start trading over $116.74 (Why? The low of $97.28 * 1.2) and it did, albeit briefly, in early December (third circle). That ended the bear market, although SPY then continued to drop, entering another bear market in July 2002, and dropping to a low of $79.95. However, that wasn't the lowest point ($78.10) which occurred after the two bear markets had ended.

As I stress in my book, **In The Money: Bear Market Strategy:**

54

The end of a bear market does not necessarily mean the beginning of a bull market.

While everyone is agreed on the start of a bear market, the definition of the start of a bull market varies widely. Some claim that a rise of 20% is enough, others stipulate that the rising prices must be over 2 months or a longer period, and Investopedia goes all out, insisting that:

The commonly accepted definition of a bull market is when stock prices rise by 20% after two declines of 20% each.

On that basis, the bull market of 2021-2022 didn't happen! For a more in depth discussion of bear markets and how to trade them I refer you to my book**: In The Money: Bear Market Strategy.**

But Did We Beat The Market?

So now we know how to tell the start and the end of a bear market, and hence when to get out of the market (at the start of the bear) and when to get back in (at the end of the bear).

This is an easy way to avoid the worst of it and does not need you to have alerts and pore over charts, just be aware that if the market is going down you need to be ready to sell your positions when it officially enters the bear.

However, the proof is in the actual figures. If we followed the IN and OUT rules above, would we have beaten the market? And how much would we have beaten it by? Let's find out.

Ch 4. Market Timing: Did It Work?

Using the Putnam study as our base, but updating it to the current date (1 November 2022) there are two investing possibilities:

- ➢ Staying fully invested
- ➢ Sitting out the bear markets

OK – so what were the results?

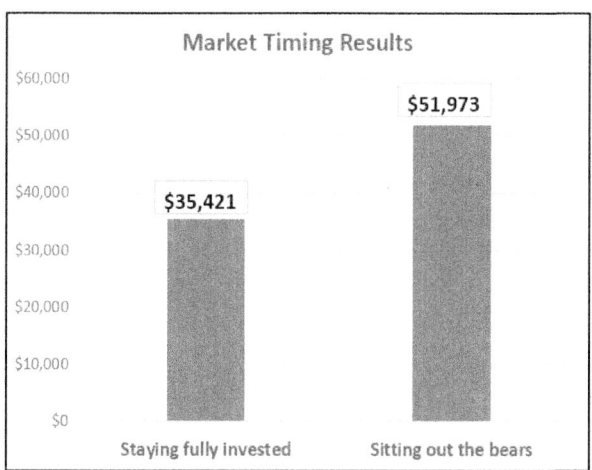

You can see that they are significantly different. You can also see that timing the market CAN work! Simply getting out of the market when a bear market started and not getting in again until the bear market ended, *makes 47% more profit.*

If we look at the ROI over the 16 years (minus one month) we get:

- ➢ Fully invested: 8.32%

- ➢ Sitting out the bears: 10.97%

Now I don't know about you, but I would rather get 11% than 8% every year!

The Cost of Bad Advice?

You **can** pay for bad advice if you want to, and many people do. But you have to ask **why** people pay financial advisers a lot of money for it. As Warren Buffet says:

Wall Street is the only place that people ride to in a Rolls Royce to get advice from those who take the subway.

Sadly, many of the people giving financial advice are not giving it from a place of experience, but from theoretical knowledge, which probably explains why around 90% of people following the advice do not make any money. No one does, but I think it is a reasonable question to ask anyone giving financial advice is *'What do you invest in and how has it performed?'*

From now on, when you hear the hoary old chestnut:

It's time in the market, not timing the market.

You will know that it is quite wrong. There IS an easy way to time the market, a way that brings significantly higher returns.

The method described in this short book is a very simple way of timing the market. There are more sophisticated ways which can bring better results, but for investors who don't have the time or inclination to watch the market every day this is effective.

You only have to watch the market when we are close to entering a bear market, and you can be sure that there will be headlines about it long before the market actually enters one.

Beating The Market

There are also ways that you not only can you time the market, but you can increase your returns by using the leverage of options. Yes, options have a bad name for being dangerous, but that reputation is unwarranted.

If you know what you are doing and use the right strategy, trading options is safer than actually owning the stock. It's like flying a plane: if someone does not know how it likely to end in disaster; however, with a trained pilot it is probably safer than driving a car.

Options are beyond the scope of this book, but if you are interested in learning about options and an easy option strategy (backtested for 30 years) then my book: In The Money: Bull Market Strategy gives a painless introduction to options, then shows how to use them to get returns that are two or three times the market returns. To find out more, visit **HeatherCullen.com.**

What You Know Now

Hopefully, the next time you hear the platitude 'It's time in the market, not timing the market' you will be able to smile to yourself because you know better. You know that the advice to buy and hold because 'you may miss the 10 best days' is very silly and, in any case, it is not telling the whole story.

You know that it is based on the ludicrous premise that someone would know in advance that the following day was going to be one of the top ten increases of the decade, even before the decade had ended. If we take an equally absurd stance and assume that we also know the top ten worst days, then the results would dramatically beat the buy and hold strategy.

You know that the logical basis of the 'stay fully invested' advice is flawed, that it is a non sequitur, a faulty conclusion.

And finally, you know that it is possible to avoid the bear markets and so increase your profits by avoiding the crushing losses that damage your portfolio with losses that take many years to recoup.

What About The Future?

Obviously, no one knows what is going to happen in the future, but as Mark Twain said:

History does not repeat itself, but it rhymes.

The best thing we can do to prepare ourselves for the future is to look at what has happened in similar situations in the past.

We have seen that the stock market is not a 'thing' made up of exchanges and stocks and options, but a mass of people, who make decisions about buying and selling based on emotions, justifying them with rational explanations after the fact.

My premise is that human nature doesn't change and hasn't changed. Investors and traders are driven by hope and fear and the stock charts are a visual representation of their hopes and fears, how strongly they are feeling them and how urgent their need for action is.

When the market goes up, they are hopeful that their investments increase in value and fearful that they may lose their profits. When the market goes down, they are fearful that their investments are losing money, but hopeful that it will turn around and they will get their money back.

Very few trading decisions are made dispassionately, and this enables us to predict what is likely to happen. Obviously, we can't predict what a single trader will do, but we can often predict what the mass of traders will do. By looking at how the market has reacted in the past we get a clue about how it will react in the future.

Timing the Market Insights

> ➢ **Time in the market IS NOT the best strategy.**
> ➢ **Timing the market IS both possible and profitable.**

We have seen that avoiding bear markets gives you much better returns than sitting through them, with the added bonus that you avoid many painful months watching your investments go down in value.

So next time your financial adviser trots out the old chestnut about time in the market you know not to take the advice!

About the Author
Heather Cullen

Heather wrote her book series In The Money and The One Hour Expert based on her 25 years of experience in the stock market. During these years, she  made hundreds of mistakes but managed to survive and to become a successful investor.

In the early years, while keeping her day job as IT Director, she was learning and trading every night. She read every book she could find on trading strategy and psychology, paid for numerous courses, subscribed to hundreds of newsletters and websites, tried every crackpot theory, and fell for the stories of every guru claiming to be making millions before breakfast.

But none of the 'trading secrets' worked more than occasionally, and the financial freedom she so desperately wanted proved to be elusive. Giving up her day job seemed like an unattainable dream.

The Impossible Dream

Over the first 15 years of trading, she made money and then lost it again. So many times! Never enough to wipe her out completely, but she wasn't able to throw up her day job and live the life of her dreams.

Although she put in many long hours of research, monitoring, and back-testing she was never consistently successful. Slowly, she realized that hard work alone did not lead to success. She saw that the ever-more-complicated strategies she was pursuing were not bringing in better results. In fact, her results were getting worse.

Euphoria and Despair

Going from euphoria to despair, often in the same month and sometimes in the same week, was exhausting. Finally, after one too many sleepless nights pacing the floor, sick with worry, she decided enough was enough.

Yet again, her stocks were plummeting, and her dreams of financial freedom disappearing. She knew she couldn't go on like that. Something had to change. She had to find a better way. She did.

The ITM Strategy

When she stepped back and looked from a different perspective, she realized the solution had been staring her in the face all the time.

It was simple and elegant - and it meant no more sleepless nights and endless hours of research.

In her first book In The Money: Bull Market Strategy, she shares with you the ITM Strategy that she uses to beat the market. It's easy and takes less than 10 minutes a week. She gives a simple set of rules that anyone, beginner or seasoned trader, can follow and be sure to beat the market and build their wealth.

You don't have to make the mistakes

In her books, Heather shares with you her rocky journey from failure to financial freedom. Her many errors and losses are not glossed over.

Instead, she openly shares them so that you don't have to make the same mistakes.

She looks on her losses as 'tuition fees' for the lessons learned, and she has paid a **lot** of tuition fees over the years. You will probably have a laugh over some of the things she has done. She can laugh **now,** but she wasn't laughing at the time as she watched her dreams of financial freedom disappearing yet again.

Today, she has not worked for twenty years, and has the financial freedom she always sought. Writing, travelling, learning and just enjoying living - it's a life she loves.

You'll Never Trade Alone

Heather writes a free weekly blog on the stock market and ITM strategy. She analyzes the charts, alerts readers if actions need to be taken and answers readers' questions. Here's the link:

HeatherCullen.com / Blog

(Or google 'Heather Cullen Blog'.)

Heather Cullen

HeatherCullen.com

Trade the tide,
not the waves

Books by Heather Cullen

In The Money Series

In The Money: Bull Market Strategy

In The Money: Overseas Edition

In The Money: Bear Market Strategy

Compare Option Strategies

One Hour Expert Series

Timing The Market

Options Trading for Beginners

Reading Stock Charts

Contact Heather Cullen

Hi! I love to hear from readers and read every email I get. I have a free weekly blog on the market and strategies, so if you have any questions or comments, please contact me there and I will happily respond. Here's the link.

HeatherCullen.com / Blog

Reviews

If you liked the **Timing The Market** I would really appreciate a review on Amazon. To find me quickly just google *'Heather Cullen Amazon Timing the Market'* and scroll down to reviews.

Thank you!

"Another lesson I learned early is that there is nothing new in Wall Street. There can't be because speculation is as old as the hills. Whatever happens in the stock market today has happened before and will happen again."

Jesse Livermore

(The original Wolf of Wall St)

Reminiscences of a Stock Operator

Printed in Dunstable, United Kingdom